# Roller Coast

by Nic Brasch
Illustrated by Adriana Puglisi

OXFORD
UNIVERSITY PRESS

My stomach was spinning like a candy floss machine.

Was I ill? No. Was I excited? Yes! I <u>certainly</u> was.

It was the school holidays, and I was going to the theme park with my best friend, Chandra.

The main character, Lily, is <u>certainly</u> excited. Can you think of another word to use instead of <u>certainly</u>? (*definitely, absolutely*)

"What shall we go on first, Lily?" Chandra asked.
"The merry-go-round!" I yelled.
We ran to the ride.

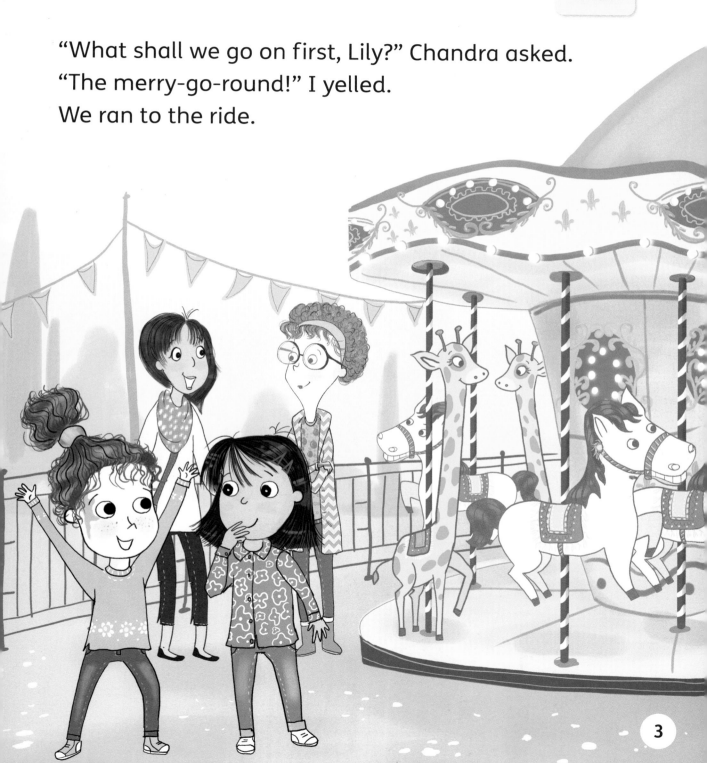

child

"Hold on tight!" I said to Chandra.
The ride started to spin, and we went around and around. Everything was a blur.

4

When we got off, Chandra tugged my arm.

"We should go on that," she said.

Chandra was looking at the roller coaster. I felt sick.

"I can't," I said, stopping before we got to the ride.

"Why not?" asked Chandra, a little confused.

I didn't want to tell her I was scared, but she was my friend. Surely she would understand?

"What is it, Lily?" she asked again.

"I don't like heights," I admitted. "You go. I don't want to stop you having fun."

I felt bad that Chandra had to go on the roller coaster without me. However, she looked very happy. She screamed so loudly I got a headache!

At last the ride finished. Chandra came to find me.
"Are you OK?" she asked gently.
"I wish I was not afraid," I said. "It looked like so much fun."

The next morning, Chandra came round with her mum.
"We have a plan to help you!" Chandra said.
They took me to a nearby park.

Chandra led me to the slide. "We'll try this first," she said.

Could I go on the slide? I wasn't sure, but Chandra kept encouraging me.

So I took a deep breath to <u>prepare</u> myself and then put my foot on the first step of the ladder. Then the next. Then the next.

Chandra came up behind me.

I went up slowly, but I made it to the top. I was amazed at how high I was!

<u>Prepare</u> means to get ready. What do you do each morning to <u>prepare</u> yourself for school?

"Now slide down," Chandra said.
"I'm not sure," I said.
"Trust me," she said. "Give it a try."
I sat down, let go ... and slid down.
"Wheeeeeeeeeee," I shouted.

The next day, Mum told me to pack my swimming bag.
"Is it my swimming lesson today?" I asked.
"You will have to wait and see," she said with a grin.

Chandra was at the swimming pool.

"Why all the mystery?" I asked her.

"I didn't want you to panic," she said.

Then I saw what Chandra wanted me to do.

There were two diving boards.

Chandra led me to the smaller one. "Let's start with this one. It's the <u>least</u> scary." She walked along it, bounced and jumped into the water.

My heart started to beat faster as I walked along the board.

Chandra was in the water below, smiling at me.

I took a deep breath ... then I jumped!

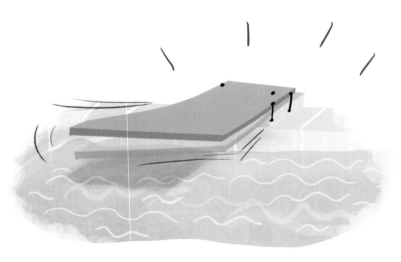

Why do you think Chandra says the smallest board is the <u>least</u> scary? What would be the opposite of <u>least</u> scary? (*most scary*)

"Now for the higher one," said Chandra.
"I can't!" I told her.
"Yes you can," Chandra said with a grin.
"Trust me!"

Chandra went first.

As I followed, I kept stopping to look down. It was not a <u>wise</u> thing to do. I felt dizzy.

"Just keep going," Chandra told me.

Lily thinks that looking down is not a <u>wise</u> thing to do.
Why do you think this isn't a <u>wise</u> idea? Can you think
of another word to use instead of <u>wise</u>? (*sensible*)

By the time I got to the top, Chandra had just
jumped in.
I went slowly, but then I jumped too. It felt like
I was flying.
I landed with a big SPLASH!

When my head popped out of the water, Chandra asked, "How was that?"

"Fantastic," I cried.

"Great! We can go home now," she said.

"No way! I'm doing that again!" I replied.

Now that I had found the <u>courage</u> to jump, I went on the diving board again ... and again ... and again!

Lily found the <u>courage</u> to jump. Have you ever felt you needed <u>courage</u> to do something?

On the last day of the holidays, Mum took Chandra and me back to the theme park.
We went to the roller coaster.

I started to feel sick again.
"You can do it, Lily," Chandra said. "You are ready."
I took a deep, shaky breath. Then I got on
and sat down.

We went up and down.
I didn't feel afraid at all!
Mum took a photo of us at the end.

When the ride ended, I said, "Thank you," to Chandra. I was so glad that she had helped me.

We started to walk home with Mum.

All of a sudden, Chandra stopped. She <u>immediately</u> jumped behind me and grabbed my arm. "Look!" she cried.

Chandra <u>immediately</u> jumped behind Lily. Why do you think she jumped straight away? How was Chandra feeling?

22

Chandra had seen a hairy spider.
"I'm afraid of spiders," she said.
"I can help you get over that," I told her.
"Trust me!"

# Retell the story